AMAZING SOCCER STORIES FOR KIDS

Exciting and Unforgettable

Soccer Adventures

- Goals, Heroes, and More!

LEIGH JORDYN

TABLE OF CONTENTS

CLAIM YOUR FREE GIFT!!!

As a way of saying thank you for your purchase, I'm offering the E-book **Play, Set, Achieve, Kids' Sports Workbook and Affirmations** for FREE to my readers!

To get instant access, just go to:

www.leighjordyn.com/free-gift

Inside the book, you will find:

1. Goal-Setting Worksheet
2. Positive Affirmation Cards
3. Word Searches
4. Mazes
5. Crossword Puzzles

INTRODUCTION

Hello young readers and superstars! I'm Leigh Jordyn, the author of "Amazing Soccer Stories for Kids," the third book in a series very close to my heart — "Amazing Sports Stories for Kids".

As a mom of three boys who absolutely adore sports, my family's love for all things athletic has been a driving force in my life. Whether on the soccer/football field or basketball court, watching my boys play their hearts out ignited a passion in me to create inspiring and motivational stories that not only entertain but also teach valuable life lessons.

In this series, I aim to transport kids into the captivating world of soccer, where they can meet relatable characters who learned the values of grit, determination, and never giving up through their love for the game. These stories are my way of sharing my family's enthusiasm for sports and instilling in young readers the same passion and dedication that soccer superstars like Lionel Messi, Cristiano Ronaldo, Pele, and Onome Ebi have shown throughout their careers.

"Amazing Soccer Stories for Kids" is a collection of heartwarming tales that blend the excitement of the game with these important life lessons, emphasizing sportsmanship and friendship. Each story is an inspiring adventure that young readers can relate to, no matter their background.

In conclusion, "Amazing Soccer Stories for Kids" is a testament to my family's love for sports and my dedication to inspiring and motivating the next generation of not just athletes but dreamers and goal-chasers. I hope you enjoy reading it as much as I enjoyed writing it!

So, let's lace up our cleats, dribble past obstacles, and aim for the goalposts. Let the stories of these remarkable soccer players be your inspiration as you pursue your own dreams. After all, the beautiful game of soccer is a great adventure, and with determination and passion, you can make every moment on the pitch count!

PELÉ

"Success is no accident. It is hard work, perseverance, learning, studying, sacrifice, and most of all, love of what you are doing or learning to do."
- Pelé

In the heart of Brazil, in the small town of Três Corações, a young boy named Edson Arantes do Nascimento was born on October 23, 1940. Little did the world know that this boy, who famously goes by the nickname Pelé, would become one of the greatest football (or soccer, as it's known in the United States) players of all time. His journey was filled with challenges and struggles, but he turned them into stepping stones on his path to success.

Pelé grew up in a poor neighborhood in Bauru. His family was far from wealthy and they lived in a small house made of wood. Pelé's father was also a soccer player who was forced to retire from the game after he fractured his leg.

Pelé helped earn extra money for his family by polishing shoes and working in tea shops as a servant. Pelé found joy in playing soccer as he used to watch his father play professionally. His family couldn't afford to buy him a soccer ball so he practiced by playing with a sock stuffed with newspaper and then tied with string! He used to play with his bare feet on the dusty streets of Bauru.

At the tender age of 11, Pelé joined a local youth team called Bauru Athletic Club. But even then, life wasn't easy. Money was tight, and he sometimes had to choose between a bus fare to practice or lunch. Yet, his talent was undeniable, and his dedication to the sport began to pay off.

With his leadership, Bauru Athletic Club's junior team managed to win the Sao Paulo state youth championship twice. At age 15, Pelé grew more confident by playing futsal with adults.

His coach and mentor, Waldemar de Brito, who was also a premier soccer player in Brazil, decided to take him for a trial at Santos in 1956. Santos Futebol Clube, or Santos FC, is a professional Brazilian football club. Waldemar had so much faith in Pelé's abilities that he even told the club's leaders that Pelé would become *"the greatest football player in the world."* Boy, was he right!

Pelé made such a strong impression that he was offered a professional contract in June of the same year. He proved himself to Santos FC when he scored a goal in his very first mainstream match against Corinthians de Santo Andre with a score of 7-1. The media was quick to predict that he would become a superstar, and he was already a regular starter when the 1957 season kicked off.

Pelé became the league's leading goal scorer in 1957 and eventually got a call to join the Brazilian national team, the Seleção Canarinha, only 10 months after starting his professional career. To this day, Pelé holds the record as the youngest player to debut for the Selecao.

In 1958, at just 17 years old, Pelé was called up to play in the FIFA World Cup. He played with the heart of a champion and scored a whopping 6 goals that day leading the Brazilian team to victory! Brazil won its first World Cup that year.

This victory made the whole world sit up and pay attention. Multiple sports clubs from other countries showed interest in having Pelé play for them. Brazil declared Pelé a national treasure thereby barring him from playing for any non-Brazilian soccer club or corporation.

Pele's journey was not without its share of injuries. In the 1962 World Cup, he suffered a severe injury that kept him out of most of the tournament. His contributions were limited but his team still won earning Pelé his 2nd World Cup. After that, he worked tirelessly to recover and came back even stronger.

Pele's greatest achievements came in the 1970 World Cup. Brazil won the tournament, and Pelé became the only player in history to win three World Cups. His skill and sportsmanship earned him admiration from fans all over the world.

Pelé wasn't just a soccer star. He was also a humanitarian. He used his fame to advocate for children's rights and promote peace. His dedication to making the world a better place was just as inspiring as his performance on the field.

After an illustrious career, Pelé retired from professional football. His legacy continued to grow as he became a global ambassador for the sport. He remained an inspiration to millions of aspiring young footballers worldwide. Pelé will be remembered as the greatest player of all time by many football fans, especially in Brazil. Cristiano Ronaldo himself is quoted as saying: *"Pelé is the greatest player in football history, and there will only be one Pelé ."*

Lessons from Pelé's Journey:

1. **Passion and determination**: You can overcome any obstacle. Even if you don't have much, if you love what you do and work hard, you can achieve greatness.
2. **Age is just a number:** Believe in your abilities, no matter your age. Pelé was just 17 when he won his first World Cup, proving that age is just a number when it comes to achieving your dreams.
3. **Resilience is the key to overcoming setbacks:** Injuries and setbacks are a part of life, but how you respond to them defines your success.

4. Give back: Use your success to make a positive impact on the world. Pele didn't just focus on his career; he also worked to make the world a better place, showing us the importance of giving back.

Pelé's life is a testament to the power of perseverance, dedication, and love for what you do. He reminds us that we can overcome any challenge and achieve greatness if we believe in ourselves and work hard.

CRISTIANO RONALDO

> *"Your love makes me strong, your hate makes me unstoppable."*
> **- Cristiano Ronaldo**

Cristiano Ronaldo is not just a famous soccer player; he's a hero who faced tough times but never gave up. In this book, we'll discover how he overcame challenges and struggles to become one of the best soccer players ever. Ronaldo's story is about working hard, never quitting, and believing that you can achieve your dreams, no matter what.

Cristiano Ronaldo was born in Portugal on February 5, 1985, in a working-class neighborhood, and is the youngest of 5 siblings. Fun fact: Cristiano Ronaldo was named after his father's favorite actor, Ronald Reagan, who was the US President at the time he was born!

Ronaldo was introduced to the world of soccer through his dad who worked as an equipment manager at a boys' club. He absolutely looked up to him and was very close to him — there was one problem, his dad drank too much. Ronaldo had often pushed and encouraged his father to stop drinking and go to rehab so he could change his ways but his father never listened. Ronaldo's mother, on the other hand, had to work as a cook and a cleaning person to make sure all the kids were fed and to keep the family's money situation steady.

When Ronaldo was a kid, he didn't have fancy soccer gear. Instead, he played with a homemade ball on the streets of his town, Funchal. Even though he didn't have much, his love for soccer made him practice daily, dribbling and shooting. By the time he was 10 years old, Ronaldo was already recognized as a phenomenon — a kid who ate, slept, and drank soccer. According to his godfather, all he wanted to do was play soccer he would miss meals or escape out of his bedroom window with a ball when he was supposed to be doing his homework!

Ronaldo had been playing with the local football club in Funchal called Nacional da liha da Madeira. He was already performing very well there so at the age of 12, he made a big decision: he left his family behind to pursue his dream of becoming a professional football player. He moved to Lisbon to join Sporting CP's youth academy, one of the biggest sports clubs in Portugal. It was a very challenging and emotional journey for such a young boy as he faced homesickness and loneliness, but he knew that this sacrifice was necessary to achieve his goals.

At age 15, Ronaldo faced an unexpected challenge. He had to go through heart surgery because of a rare problem called tachycardia. This meant that his heart would beat very fast even when he was resting. It made people worry about whether he could keep playing soccer. Fortunately, the surgery was minor and very successful, and after a quick rest, Ronaldo was back on the soccer field.

After a fantastic season with Sporting that caught the eye of the biggest football clubs in Europe, Ronaldo joined the famous English team Manchester United in 2003. He became a sensation right away and quickly earned a reputation as one of the top forwards in the sport. Manchester offered him £12 million to sign him — he was only 16 years old then! This was definitely a record fee for a player his age.

The challenges didn't stop for Ronaldo. In 2005, when he was already playing for Manchester United, his father died from alcohol-related kidney problems; then in 2007, his mother struggled with breast cancer. These years were deeply challenging periods in his life, but he continued to perform at the highest level.

In 2009, Ronaldo made a record-breaking move to Real Madrid for a then-world-record transfer fee. The pressure to perform at the highest level was immense, but Ronaldo thrived under the spotlight. He shattered goal-scoring records, won numerous titles, and became a global icon.

In 2018, Ronaldo made a surprising move to Juventus, an Italian club. At an age when many footballers started to decline, Ronaldo continued to excel. He faced the challenge of adapting to a new league and continued to prove that age is just a number.

Ronaldo's impact extends beyond the football field. He's known for his charity work, including donations to children's hospitals and disaster relief efforts. He also serves as a role model for young athletes worldwide.

Cristiano Ronaldo's journey from the streets of Madeira to the pinnacle of world football is an inspiring tale of dedication, hard work, and resilience — and a lot of risk-taking! His life is a testament to the fact that challenges and struggles are not roadblocks but stepping stones to success.

Lessons from Ronaldo's Journey:

1. **Passion Knows No Boundaries:** Ronaldo's story teaches us that true passion can drive us to overcome obstacles and limitations. Even after going through a heart condition at such a young age, and going through surgery to fix it, Ronaldo never let go of his dream.
2. **Sacrifice and Determination:** Ronaldo's willingness to leave his comfort zone teaches us that achieving greatness often requires making sacrifices and stepping out of our comfort zones.

3. **Embrace Change and Adapt:** Ronaldo's story shows us that adapting to change and pushing our limits is essential for growth and success. Change is the only constant thing in this world.

4. **Perseverance in the Face of Adversity:** Ronaldo's ability to persevere through personal hardships teaches us that determination can help us navigate even the toughest times in our lives.

5. **Set Goals and Break Records:** Ronaldo's relentless pursuit of excellence teaches us that setting ambitious goals and working tirelessly to achieve them can lead to incredible accomplishments.

6. **Age Is Not a Limitation:** Ronaldo's ability to perform at the highest level well into his 30s reminds us that age should never be a barrier to pursuing our dreams. This goes both ways — there is no such thing as "too young" or "too old", if you have a dream, go for it!

7. **Giving Back and Being a Role Model:** Ronaldo's commitment to making a positive impact on the world teaches us the importance of using our success to help others.

So, as you chase your dreams, remember one of Cristiano Ronaldo's famous words: *"Don't let small obstacles get in the way of being victorious. Remember you are stronger than the challenges you face."* Let his story be a source of inspiration as you face your own challenges and strive for greatness in whatever path you choose to follow.

DIEGO MARADONA

"When you win, you don't get carried away. But if you go step by step, with confidence, you can go far."
- **Diego Maradona**

Diego Armando Maradona was born on October 30, 1960, in Villa Fioritio, a slum in the Buenos Aires suburbs of Argentina. It was a very poor neighborhood where houses were collapsing and garbage was everywhere. Drugs and violence were rampant in Diego's surroundings.

Diego was the fifth of eight children in a poor but very close-knit family. Life was often tough and uncertain. His father was a factory worker who worked hard to earn enough money to feed his large family. His mother, on the other hand, stayed at home to look after all the children as well as educate them.

Their family was so poor that the majority of the time, there wasn't enough food for the whole family to eat. Diego's mother had to pretend she couldn't eat anything because her stomach hurt so bad! It wasn't true and Diego found this out later on. She just had to do that to make sure the children were able to eat a proper dinner.

Another sacrifice that Diego's parents made was saving up enough money to buy Diego a soccer ball for his 3rd birthday. This turned out to be the biggest blessing for their family and was what started Diego's path to soccer stardom!

Diego's love for football was evident from a young age. He spent hours honing his skills on the streets of Villa Fiorito, using a ragged ball and makeshift goalposts. These challenging circumstances forced him to develop his incredible dribbling skills, close ball control, and footballing instincts. Little did he know that these very streets would be the training ground for his future greatness.

At age eight, Diego joined Las Cebollitas ("The Little Onions"), a boys' soccer team that went on to win 136 consecutive games and a national championship.

At age 14, he joined the junior team of Argentinos Juniors. His talent quickly caught the eye of scouts and coaches. However, this journey was not without its difficulties. Diego faced doubts and hate from some of the club managers and parents of other players. Diego had a short stature but was more muscular than other kids his age and they accused him of being older than his age. His mother had to present his birth certificate to prove his age!

The hatred didn't end there. Diego was a force to be reckoned with. He was so good on the field with his strong legs and exceptional techniques that none of his opponents could beat him or steal the ball from him. This made his opponents' parents angry and they proceeded to insult him, calling him a "dirty rat" and "dark skin".

Do you know how Diego responded to these insults hurled at him? He didn't fight back or get mad at them — neither did he give up. He responded on the pitch. He only had one aim — to score goals. The hatred from doubters transformed him internally and made him an even better and more competitive player.

At this point in time, young Diego already realized that soccer was the only way he could help his family fight poverty. He was determined to work hard to achieve this and knew that talent alone wasn't enough.

The Argentino Juniors' club managers also saw this talent and determination in Diego and wanted to make him an even stronger player. He had to train twice as hard in order to achieve this. Diego and his father spent hours navigating from one bus to another every day, after his father's work, just to get to the soccer club for training.

At age 15, the club decided to house Diego in an apartment near the club to make training easier and more accessible. It was also at this time that Diego received his first paycheck! What a proud moment that must have been! He bought a TV for his parents from that first paycheck. From then on, he was able to help his family live a more comfortable life. One of his brothers, Lalo, was quoted saying *"At 15, Diego became like another father for us. He made our day-to-day lives much more comfortable."*

Diego's goal was to buy a new house for his parents and he knew in order for him to do that, he needed to move up to the pro ranks. Only 10 days before he turned 16, Diego signed with the Argentine First Division making him the youngest in history to do. Two weeks after his 16th birthday, just a few moments after coming onto the pitch, he scored his first professional goal and the crowd went wild!

Four months later, Diego made his debut with the national team, becoming the youngest Argentine ever to do so. He has then moved to different football clubs and has made World Cup appearances in 1982, 1986, 1990, and 1994.

The 1986 FIFA World Cup in Mexico is where Maradona truly left his mark. In the quarter-final match against England, he scored two of the most iconic goals in football history — the "Hand of God" and the "Goal of the Century." These moments of brilliance showcased his unparalleled skill and determination to succeed.

Despite his on-field success, Diego Maradona battled with personal demons. He faced numerous controversies, including struggles with drug addiction and weight issues.

These challenges threatened to overshadow his incredible talent and tarnish his legacy.

Diego Maradona's influence extended far beyond football. He used his fame and fortune to support charitable causes and help those in need. His legacy continues to inspire generations of footballers and fans around the world.

Lessons from Diego's Journey:

1. **Embrace Your Roots:** Diego's story teaches us that your humble beginnings do not define your future. It's where you aim and how hard you work that truly matters. Diego also never forgot where he came from and continued to represent Villa Fiorita.

2. **Turn Challenges into Opportunities:** Diego's story encourages us to see obstacles as stepping stones to success. Instead of complaining about the lack of resources, he used it as an opportunity to develop his unique style of play.

3. **Perseverance in the Face of Adversity:** Diego's life teaches us that setbacks are a part of every journey. It's your determination to get back up and keep going that defines your character.

4. **Believe in Yourself:** Diego's story reminds us that self-belief can move mountains. When you have faith in your abilities, you can achieve the extraordinary.

5. **Seek Help and Never Give Up:** Maradona's life teaches us that it's okay to ask for help when facing personal challenges. The journey to self-improvement may be difficult, but it's worth it.

6. **Give Back:** Diego's story encourages us to use our success and influence to make the world a better place.

Diego Maradona's life was a testament to the power of dreams, determination, and resilience. From the poverty-stricken streets of Villa Fiorito to the heights of footballing greatness, he faced challenges head-on and emerged victorious. As you embark on your own journey through life, remember the valuable lessons from the life of Diego Maradona. No matter how tough the road may seem, with the right attitude and unwavering determination, you too can achieve greatness and leave a lasting legacy.

"Life is like a game of soccer. You need goals. If there are no goals in your life, you can't win." - Diego Maradona

ONOME EBI

"I am a super strong woman, I am powerful, I am extraordinary, I am a queen, I am a fighter, I am a goal getter, I am unique, I am a football player, I am ME".
- **Onome Ebi**

Onome Ebi, a name that resonates with strength and determination. Her life story is a beacon of inspiration, a testament to what one can achieve through perseverance and hard work. Onome's journey is one filled with challenges and struggles that have shaped her into the remarkable individual she is today.

Onome was born on May 8, 1983, in Lagos, Lagos State, Nigeria to an Urhobo family. The Urhobo is a major ethnic group in Delta State, Nigeria. Her name Onome means *"My Own"*.

Just like most African superstar athletes, Onome came from humble beginnings. She comes from a Christian family and is one of ten siblings. Her parents didn't want her to play soccer, just like the rest of society, they see soccer as a sport for men. Onome's parents really wanted her to stop playing and focus on her education.

Onome was practically born a footballer as she claimed she started playing soccer while she was still in her mother's womb. She started playing for the female soccer team in her secondary school in Ajegunle, an area known to be the slums of Lagos State. During these days, Onome's school had a Principals Cup football competition and Onome always performed very well, exhibiting her skills for everyone to see!

In 2001, she gained the attention of the team manager of Omidiran Babes in Osogbo, which is a different town in Nigeria, and that was the first ever soccer club that she joined. 4 years later, another soccer club named Bayelsa Queens showed interest in her and she ended up playing with them for 3 years before she moved on to playing professionally.

At this point, Onome's parents were still not on board with Onome taking soccer seriously. They were worried that playing soccer professionally would mean leaving her studies behind or not finishing as she had to go to training and competitions. They wouldn't allow her to go on trips to play and Onome even fell sick from possible depression because of this. Her parents had to take her to the hospital but the doctors couldn't figure out what was wrong with her — only that her heart was heavy. She was in the hospital for 5 days and her parents eventually allowed her to go on trips. Onome was also able to prove to them that she was determined to excel both in her studies and in the pitch.

The battle against gender stereotypes became a defining struggle for Onome. She had to fight for every opportunity and prove herself again and again. Coaches and teammates soon realized that her dedication and skill transcended gender, and she earned her place on various teams.

The journey was challenging, but Onome's spirit was unbreakable. She demonstrated that girls could excel in traditionally male-dominated sports. Her story became a source of inspiration for many young girls who aspired to break free from societal constraints.

Onome's dedication and talent eventually led her to the Nigerian Women's National Team, where she faced even more formidable challenges. The competition was fierce, and making it to the national team was a dream come true. But the real struggle was only beginning.

Traveling to other countries, playing in high-pressure matches, and representing her nation were tremendous responsibilities. The road was fraught with hardships, from injuries to the intense physical and mental demands of professional football. Onome never backed down from a challenge, consistently putting in her best effort and pushing her boundaries.

Aside from the fact that Onome has to play in a male-dominated sport, she also has to defend her ability to still play at her age. Right now, in 2023, Onome turned 40 years old and still going strong! She continues to be incredibly athletic, and her skill and swiftness still surpass those of many younger players joining the field.

Onome is now known as one of Nigeria's most accomplished and famous female soccer players. She achieved something amazing! She is the very first African player, both man and woman, to participate in the World Cup six times! Plus, she's the one Nigerian player that fans are super excited to take pictures with.

Back in Nigeria, Onome is always finding new ways to help others through charity and community projects. She has her own foundation that's all about supporting young girls who dream of becoming professional soccer players, and she also works hard to support Nigeria's female soccer league, which really needs a hand. On top of all that, she gives 1% of her earnings to Common Goal, a project that helps important organizations use soccer to make the world a better place.

Lessons from Onome Ebi's Journey:

1. **Resilience:** No matter how tough the journey, resilience is the key to success. Onome's life is a testament to the power of bouncing back from setbacks and staying strong in the face of adversity.

2. **Determination:** Onome's unwavering commitment to her dream of playing football is a reminder that with determination, there's no dream too big to achieve.

3. **Overcoming Gender Stereotypes:** She broke through societal expectations and showed that passion and talent are not limited by gender. Every young girl should believe in herself and pursue her dreams, no matter what they may be.

4. **Global Ambassadorship:** Onome's journey reminds us that the impact of our actions can transcend borders. We all have the potential to inspire and motivate others.

Onome Ebi's life is a true story of resilience, determination, and the triumph of the human spirit. From a young girl facing gender stereotypes in Nigeria to a global ambassador for women's soccer, her journey is an inspiration to all. She teaches us that no matter what challenges we face, our dreams are worth the fight. Through hard work, dedication, and the unwavering support of loved ones, we can overcome any obstacle.

KATAYOUN KHOSROWYAR

"In time, I hope to create something more sustainable within women's soccer, so that I can help millions rather than just a couple of hundred ".

- **Katayoun Khosrowyar**

Katayoun "Kat" Khosrowyar was born and raised in Tulsa, Oklahoma by her Iranian father and grandmother. She has also spent some time in Houston, and has a master's degree in chemical engineering from the University of Birmingham in the United Kingdom. She likes to call herself a "Midwest girl.

When Kat was only 5 years old, her father encouraged her to participate in sports. She spent her time playing with her sisters, joining in games with her dad, and anyone who would play with her. For Kat, this was a natural path to her development. In fact, her football journey began even before she had the ability to make such a decision for herself, all thanks to her supportive father.

The sports community, specifically soccer, has always surrounded Kat. In high school, she was already playing at a high level, traveling from one state to another across the US. She has also participated in numerous competitions, hoping to play at a national level one day. Who would have thought that her dream would come true but only, it'll be on a pitch halfway across the world?!

When Kat was 16 years old, she went on a family vacation to Iran. That was her first time to set foot in her grandmother's home country. While on vacation, her skills in soccer were noticed and she was invited to join the Iranian women's national *futsal* team — the first such team since the 70's revolution. *Futsal* is a type of soccer that is played indoors on a much smaller court. Even though she didn't know the language, Kat's background and determination to always strive for success made her decide to move to Tehran and start a whole new life!

Before 1979, soccer was a popular sport in Iran, but because of strict rules that said all women had to wear a headscarf in public, Iranian women were only allowed to compete in rifle shooting for over 20 years. This was known as the 70's revolution. Things started to change when students from Alzahra University in Tehran created a futsal team in the early 1990s, and then a national league was formed. In 2005, Jordan invited Iran to send a team to play in the West Asian Championships, and that's when the brand new national team was born.

When Kat first arrived in Tehran, there were no soccer teams or even soccer fields, much less coaches. After a few months, a national team was formed due to the West Asian Championships. FIFA began to support Iranian women in competitions. New gyms and sports arenas started to open. It was an amazing time for sports in Iran, especially for girls who loved soccer. The women who played soccer before the big changes were made in 1979 stepped up to help the new generation of kids get into sports!

When Kat moved from the United States to play for Iran, she had to make a lot of changes and follow new rules, like the one that said women had to wear the hijab. While Kat was playing for the Iranian Women's Team in 2011, their team made it to the second round of the Olympic qualifications. But right before their next match, a FIFA person told them they couldn't play because they were wearing the hijab! It was such a sad and unfair moment.

This incident lit up a fire in Kat and she started a campaign called "Let Us Play." She wanted FIFA to understand that girls should be allowed to wear the hijab while playing soccer. And in 2014, the campaign worked! FIFA finally said it was okay for girls to wear head coverings for religious reasons. This was a huge moment for women soccer players all around the world!

This situation also made Kat focus on making the hijab better for girls to play in. She changed how it's designed and the materials used to make it more comfortable. She explained, *"I learned about how clothes work with your body, so I made the hijab less tight around the neck, more supportive around the ears, and even added a cooling system."*

With these helpful changes, Kat wanted to show other teams that they were strong and capable, even with the hijab.

In 2013, Kat decided to stop playing soccer after eight years. During those eight years, she helped Iran's team go from being at the very bottom of FIFA's rankings to being in the top 50. She had already thought about what she wanted to do next in her career. She wanted to coach and empower women in sports instead!

Kat became the first woman from the Middle East to earn a FIFA A-license and was coaching two of Iran's youth teams. She also became a speaker and even did a TED talk in 2015 called *"Empowering Women Through Sports."*

Kat changed the game for girls all over Iran. She worked very hard to make her teams even better at soccer and made sure that girls in Iran get more chances to play. She wanted people to see them as soccer players first, not just as girls who wear the hijab.

Lessons from Kat's Journey:

1. **Embrace Your Passion:** No matter the challenges, embrace your passion with unwavering determination. Kat's love for football was her guiding light, and she never let anyone dim it. She shone wherever she went, even if it was halfway across the world.

2. **Break Stereotypes:** Kat showed that stereotypes are just barriers that can be broken down. Don't be afraid to challenge societal norms and expectations if they stand in the way of your dreams.

3. **Perseverance Pays Off:** Kat's journey wasn't easy, but her unwavering perseverance allowed her to rise above every obstacle. If you believe in your dreams, keep moving forward despite the challenges.

4. **Be a Trailblazer:** Don't be afraid to be a pioneer. Kat's appointment as the head coach of the Iranian Women's National Team was a historic moment. By breaking new ground, you can inspire others to follow in your footsteps.

5. **Empower Others:** Kat's dedication to improving women's football in Iran shows the importance of empowering others. Use your success as a platform to help those who aspire to achieve their dreams.

Kat's story is a testament to the power of determination, resilience, and unwavering belief in one's dreams. Her journey from a young girl in Tulsa, OK to a pioneering football coach in Tehran, Iran is an inspiration to us all. Kat's life tells us that no dream is too big, and no challenge is too great if you are determined to achieve your goals.

In the face of adversity and societal norms, Kat rose above the challenges and made a lasting impact on the world of football. Her story is a beacon of hope for young girls and boys alike, reminding us that with passion, perseverance, and a willingness to challenge the status quo, we can achieve our dreams.

As you close the final pages of Kat's remarkable journey, remember the lessons she leaves behind. Kat's story is a reminder that you, too, can be an unstoppable dreamer, just like her!

CARLOS TEVEZ

"I don't fear failure – I see it as an opportunity to learn and improve."
- Carlos Tevez

Carlos Tevez, a name synonymous with grit, determination, and the indomitable spirit of a true champion, emerged from humble beginnings to conquer the world of football. His life is a remarkable testament to the power of unwavering self-belief, hard work, and resilience in the face of adversity.

Tevez was born Carlos Alberto Martínez on February 5, 1984 in Ciudadela, Buenos Aires. He grew up in the neighborhood of Ejército de Los Andes, better known as Fuerte Apache, a town now known as one of the most dangerous places in the world with a high rate of children going missing before they reach their teenage years. This was also where Carlos got his nickname of "El Apache".

If there's one thing the people of Fuerte Apache loved, it was soccer! Some local teams formed a crime-free space for young kids to be able to develop their love for the sport. In the early 90s, two names stood out to really have potential in the game. One of them was Carlos! He attracted attention not just because of his amazing skills but also because of the huge scar on his neck.

This deep scar is from a third-degree burn and extends from his face, neck, and down to his chest. An incident happened involving boiling water when Carlos was just 10 months old. It was so severe that he had to stay in the ICU for about 2 months.

The worst part? Carlos was abandoned by his single mother who couldn't handle him with these injuries. Young Carlos was adopted by his mother's sister and her husband Segundo Tevez. Carlos eventually changed his surname to Tevez.

Soccer was Tevez's escape from the difficulties of his childhood. He displayed remarkable talent from an early age, often playing with makeshift footballs on the dusty streets of Ciudadela. His passion for the sport was unstoppable.

Tevez's journey to professional football was not without its challenges. Despite his talent, he faced rejection from several clubs. But he never gave up. In 2001, at 16 years old, Carlos joined Boca Juniors, a renowned Argentine club, where he honed his skills.

Tevez's move to Brazil to play for Corinthians in 2005 was a significant milestone. He faced cultural differences, language barriers, and homesickness. However, his sheer determination and ability to adapt allowed him to succeed.

In 2006, Tevez made the leap to European football by signing with West Ham United in England. His early days in the Premier League were tough, and his club faced a relegation battle. However, Tevez's resilience shone through as he scored crucial goals to keep West Ham in the top flight.

Tevez's career continued to soar as he joined Manchester United in 2007. He played a pivotal role in the team's success, winning several titles, including the UEFA Champions League. His determination, work ethic, and ability to perform on the grandest stages inspired millions of fans worldwide.

Despite his success in Europe, Tevez remained connected to his roots. In 2015, he returned to Boca Juniors, fulfilling a lifelong dream. His homecoming was met with immense enthusiasm, and he continued to excel on the pitch.

Carlos Tevez's remarkable journey from the streets of Ciudadela to the pinnacle of world football is a testament to the power of perseverance, determination, and self-belief. His life story teaches us invaluable lessons.

Lessons from Carlos' Journey:

1. **Humble Beginnings Do Not Define You:** Carlos' early life reminds us that our origins don't dictate our future. No matter where you come from, it's your determination and hard work that can change your destiny. Carlos refused to let his circumstances limit his dreams.

2. **Find Your Passion and Pursue It Relentlessly:** Carlos' passion for football became his driving force. Discovering what you love and pursuing it with unwavering determination is the first step toward achieving greatness.

3. **Rejection is Not Failure:** Carlos' story teaches us that rejection is just a detour, not the end of the road. It's a part of the journey towards success. Keep pushing forward, and your breakthrough will come.

4. **Embrace Change and Adaptability:** Carlos' ability to adapt to new environments demonstrates the importance of being open to change. In life, we often encounter situations that require us to adapt and grow. Embrace these challenges as opportunities for personal growth.

5. **Thrive Under Pressure:** Carlos' performances under pressure illustrate the value of remaining calm and focused when facing adversity. Pressure is an opportunity to rise and showcase your true potential.

6. **Consistency and Hard Work Pay Off:** Carlos' journey to superstardom reinforces the notion that sustained effort and dedication yield rewards. Success is not a one-time achievement; it's a product of consistent hard work.

These lessons are not just applicable to the world of football but to every aspect of life. Carlos Tevez's story serves as an inspiration to young readers, showing them that with unwavering determination, they can overcome any obstacle and achieve their dreams. No matter where you come from, your dreams are within reach if you have the heart to pursue them. Carlos Tevez's life is a shining example of what can be achieved through hard work and an unshakeable belief in oneself.

SADIO MANE

"Challenges are what make life interesting, overcoming them is what makes life meaningful." –
Sadio Mane

Sadio Mane, the pride of Senegal, is a football superstar who has captured the hearts of fans all over the world. His journey from a humble village in Africa to the grand stadiums of Europe is a story of unwavering determination, resilience, and the relentless pursuit of dreams.

Sadio Mane was born on April 10, 1992, in the very small village of Bambali, deep in the south of Senegal. Sadio came to football later than most, he was banned from playing as a kid by his dad who wanted him to focus on religion. His father passed away at age 7 and he lived with his uncle.

From an early age, Sadio's path was filled with obstacles. He started off just playing in the streets. Later on, he wanted to play more seriously but the nearest football pitch was miles away from his village. He would often run the distance barefoot to reach the local football academy for training. The lack of proper equipment, training facilities, and even food didn't deter him. He'd wake up before sunrise and train until late in the evening, perfecting his skills and nurturing his passion for the game.

Despite facing numerous obstacles and financial constraints, he never gave up on his dreams and worked incredibly hard to make a name for himself in the football world. According to Sadio, *"When I was young, I only thought about the*

Premier League, which I watched on TV. Only Premier League. It was a big dream for me."

During the 2002 World Cup, his country, Senegal, got to the quarter-finals in their first appearance at the showpiece. Beating holders in France in the opening match was a miracle he never forgot. This ignited Sadio's obsession with the sport and to become a soccer player even more! Since then, Sadio and his friends started having tournaments in their village. He became more and more determined to be the best and win every game.

Their whole village would cheer on him as he became the best among all the players. His family, on the other hand, wasn't too keen on soccer — they were all very big on religion and didn't understand the obsession with the sport.

As Sadio kept playing, his family started to see how serious and passionate he was about soccer. He was finally able to convince his family, especially his uncle, to allow him to move to a local town, and eventually to Dakar City, which is his country's capital. They even helped raise money for Sadio to make this big move there! Some other people in their village who witnessed Sadio's talent also helped raise money, they believed he had the best possible shot to pursue and succeed in soccer.

In Dakar City, Sadio lived in the suburbs with a family that he didn't even know. He offered to pay a little bit of rent and explained his reason for needing to be there. Luckily, the family took him in and did everything they could to make sure Sadio could just focus on soccer.

Sadio found the most popular soccer club in Dakar and went over the next day to try out. He was one of so many players who were there. The coach saw him come in, looked him up and down, and asked him if he was in the right place! Sadio went there wearing a pair of old and torn boots and a pair of old shorts that were not fit to play soccer! He didn't look like he belonged there!

Sadio answered the coach saying he came in with his best clothes and he just wanted to play and show them what he got. Nevertheless, the coach allowed him to try out and boy was he in for a surprise! Sadio performed like a pro! After the tryouts, the coach came over and told Sadio he's picking him to be part of the team! Sadio has become a part of the local soccer team academy.

Living far from home in difficult conditions, Sadio faced a constant struggle. He had to balance school, football, and work, doing various odd jobs to support himself. Yet, he never lost sight of his goal, practicing relentlessly and making the most of every opportunity.

Sadio's success and obvious talent at the club did not go unnoticed. At the age of 19, he was offered a chance to join the French club, FC Metz. This was a dream come true, but the challenges continued. Mane faced language barriers, cultural differences, and the pressure of performing at a higher level.

His early years in European football were tough, marked by rejection and self-doubt. He moved from club to club, including Red Bull Salzburg and Southampton, always facing challenges but never losing hope. His work ethic, humility, and unwavering belief in himself caught the attention of scouts and managers.

In 2016, Sadio Mane made a life-changing move to Liverpool FC, one of the most prestigious clubs in the world. This was a momentous step in his career, but it came with immense pressure. Liverpool fans are known for their passion, and expectations were high.

Sadio rose to the occasion, quickly becoming a fan favorite with his blistering pace, skill, and unyielding determination. In his first season, he helped Liverpool secure a spot in the UEFA Champions League, and the following year, they reached the final. Mane's never-give-up attitude and ability to rise to the occasion made him a vital part of the team.

Sadio's journey was far from smooth, and he faced setbacks as well. In 2019, during a critical part of the season, he suffered a severe injury that required surgery. It was a heartbreaking moment for him, but he didn't let it break his spirit. He worked tirelessly to recover, never losing sight of his dream to help Liverpool win titles. His resilience paid off when Liverpool clinched the Premier League and the Champions League titles.

Sadio's influence extends far beyond the football field. He is not only a national hero but also a philanthropist. He has donated millions of dollars to build schools, hospitals, and infrastructure in Senegal, giving back to his community and inspiring the youth of his country to chase their dreams.

Lessons from Sadio's Journey:

1. **Dream Big:** Sadio's journey began with a simple dream. Don't be afraid to dream big and set ambitious goals for yourself.
2. **Work Hard:** Sadio's success is a result of his relentless work ethic. No dream is too big if you're willing to put in the effort.
3. **Persevere:** Obstacles are a part of every journey. Sadio's ability to persevere through hardships is a reminder that setbacks can lead to comebacks.

4. **Believe in Yourself:** Self-belief is a powerful force. Sadio's unwavering belief in his abilities helped him overcome countless challenges.

5. **Give Back:** Sadio Mane's commitment to giving back to his community showcases the importance of helping others when you achieve success.

Sadio Mane's story is a remarkable tale of a young boy from a small village in Senegal who conquered the world of soccer. His life is an inspiration for children and young adults facing obstacles in their pursuit of dreams. Sadio's journey teaches us that no dream is too big, no obstacle too great, and no challenge insurmountable. With hard work, determination, and self-belief, we can overcome adversity and achieve our goals, just like the Lion of Senegal, Sadio Mane.

VICTOR MOSES

"I have always believed in the ability that I have got."
— **Victor Moses**

Victor Moses was born on December 12, 1990, in Lagos, Nigeria. He was the son of a Christian pastor named Austine Moses and his wife, Josephine Moses. They were both missionaries in Kaduna State. Victor was raised with strong Christian beliefs, which became the most important part of his life as he grew up. During his entire childhood, Victor joined his parents as they talked about God's teachings to many people, sharing their faith with crowds.

In the year 2000, a religious riot broke out involving Christians and Muslims in Kaduna State, Nigeria. This was known as the Kaduna riot which lasted for 3 months. Around 5000 deaths were recorded – sadly, among them were Victor's parents. Young Victor was only 11 years old when this happened.

Luckily for Victor, he wasn't at home when this whole thing happened. He was away, playing soccer with his friends in a distant town. He felt really scared and devastated when he heard what had happened to his parents.

Being the son of a Christian pastor, Victor's friends have heard that he might be the next target. They hid him for about a week to keep him safe. Luckily, the British government intervened to calm the situation down. They also accepted a few refugees from Kaduna and Victor was one of those that were accepted. He traveled to England and sought asylum with the help and support of his uncle. An asylum seeker is someone who has fled their home in search of safety and protection in another country. A family from South London accepted the responsibility to take care of him.

Victor's move to England wasn't without its difficulties. He experienced homesickness and cultural shock, but he also rekindled his passion and dream to play soccer and become a soccer star. He embraced the challenges, knowing that they were all part of his journey to success.

In the UK, Victor went to Stanley Technical High School (now known as Harris Academy) and played for the school's soccer club. He was performing very well for the team and was scouted by the Cosmos 90 FC in a nearby league called the Tandridge League.

While playing there for quite some time, some special soccer scouts from Crystal Palace FC saw him play and asked him to join their team at the Selhurst Park stadium, which was really close to his school. Moses became well-known at the age of 14 when he scored more than 100 goals for Crystal Palace's under-14 team. In one of the games, he even scored all 5 goals for the team! He has helped the club win several cups.

Victor's path to professional soccer wasn't a straightforward one. After joining Chelsea FC, he went on multiple loan spells to various clubs to gain experience. These loan spells were often in different cities and countries, which meant adapting to new environments, languages, and playing styles.

These experiences taught him to be adaptable and resilient. Victor said, *"Every challenge is an opportunity to learn and grow. Embrace change, and you'll become a better player and person."*

Victor Moses's big break came when he returned to Chelsea FC in the 2016-2017 season. He was reimagined as a right wing-back, a position that showcased his speed, dribbling skills, and work rate. Under the management of Antonio Conte, Victor became an integral part of the Chelsea squad, helping the team win the Premier League that season.

During this whole time playing for the teams in the UK, Victor has been wanting to go back to his homeland of Nigeria. He has applied to switch nationality but it went through several issues, mostly awaiting England's approval. FIFA, the group that makes the rules for soccer, took a bit of time, but they eventually gave their approval after saying no a few times. Finally, in November 2011, they said it was okay for him to play for Nigeria.

Victor represented the Nigerian national team. He played a key role in helping Nigeria qualify for the 2018 FIFA World Cup. His performances on the international stage inspired a new generation of Nigerian soccer players and fans.

Victor never forgot where he came from and often reflected on his childhood memories playing soccer in the streets of Kaduna. *"I wore no shoes. We simply barefooted, and when a small ball fell at our feet and we started out playing football,"* said Victor.

Lessons from Victor's Journey:

1. **Never Give Up:** No matter how tough life gets, keep pushing forward. Victor's journey is a testament to the fact that determination can overcome adversity.

2. **Embrace Challenges:** Challenges are opportunities in disguise. Embrace them, learn from them, and use them to grow stronger. Victor was devastated about his parent's deaths but he used that to push himself to succeed in soccer.

3. **Believe in Yourself:** When others doubt you, believe in yourself. Victor's belief in his own abilities helped him achieve his dreams.

4. **Adaptability:** Life is full of changes. Victor's ability to adapt to new environments and challenges made him a better player and person. He had to adapt living in a whole new country with a different culture and even language. Having to move to different soccer teams, Victor still adapted to all the different club cultures and rules.

5. **Dream Big:** No dream is too big. Victor's journey from the streets of Kaduna to the Premier League is proof that with hard work, anything is possible.

Victor's life story is an incredible tale of a young boy who faced adversity with courage and determination. From the humble streets of Kaduna to the grand stadiums of the Premier League, his journey is an inspiration to all. Victor's story teaches us that with unwavering determination, we can overcome life's challenges and achieve our dreams. It's a reminder that, like him, you can transform your life through grit and determination.

SABITRA BHANDARI

"From the money I have earned, I want to spend for the education of my brothers and sisters."
- Sabitra Bhandari

Sabitra's life is a testament to the power of determination, hard work, and unwavering belief in one's dreams. Born into humble beginnings in the small village of Lamjung District of Nepal, Sabitra faced challenges and struggles that would have deterred many. But she defied the odds and rose to become a renowned international soccer player, inspiring millions along the way.

Sabitra's love for football ignited at an early age. She watched local boys play, yearning to join them. Despite societal expectations, her parents recognized her passion and encouraged her to play. Nothing could stop her from dreaming big. She wanted to become a teammate of then Nepal women's stars Anu Lama and Jamuna Gurung.

Sabitra is the 2nd of 6 children and her father was the sole breadwinner. Life was hard for their family. Sabitra didn't have the heart to ask for a football from her father. She never asked for a kit or soccer boots either.

She started playing at the age of 12 but because she didn't have any football at home, she would make her own by stuffing plastic inside socks and using that to kick around as a soccer ball!

At that time, women never played soccer as it wasn't accepted in society yet. Sabitra would often go out and play with the boys in the neighborhood. She would play barefoot as she had no proper shoes for it. Some boys would offer her a pair but they often turned out to be too big for her and she felt like she could play better without them.

Sabitra started to join some girls' competitions where she quickly became the top scorer and performer. In 2014, a national referee noticed her exceptional soccer skills, got her number, and called her 2 months later to inform her about a club trial.

That was a difficult decision for Sabrita to make. The trial was in Kathmandu – a seven-hour bus journey from Lamjung. She was worried about the money needed for the travel and also, she had to buy boots for the trial. Sabitra hesitantly spoke with her father who blessed her and handed over the money. If there's one thing Sabrita had going for her, it was the support from her family, especially her father.

She performed very well at the soccer trial and was offered a contract with Nepal APF Club. This was the breakthrough that she needed and was what started her career in soccer. Her performance at the club level soon got her a national team call up and since then, Sabrita has not looked back.

At the club, Sabrita now has proper soccer equipment and gear, including boots. A lot of national players also belonged to that club, including her idols Lama and Gurung! This is a dream come true for Sabrita! She enjoyed playing and training with them and has said that they have taught her a lot.

That same year, Sabrita made the Nepal team for the 2014 South Asian Football Federation Championship. This was her international debut against Bhutan. She was sent onto the pitch as a sub and ended up scoring a goal sealing an 8-0 victory!

In the next couple of years, Sabrita's popularity really rose as everyone started to really notice and know her and what she was capable of on the pitch. Sabrita finished the 2016 regional championship as top scorer with 12 goals as Nepal reached the last four. She was also the top scorer in the 2019 SAFF Championship.

Sabrita has been incredible and extraordinary, scoring 43 goals in 41 matches. All those wins came with a price though. Sabrita hurt her knee, tearing her ACL in 2021 during a Women's National League match. She couldn't play for a year and that made her very anxious! She wasn't sure if she'd ever be able to play soccer again. With determination, Sabrita worked hard during therapy, bounced back, and had a game lined up already.

In one of her games in India, the head coach of a men's soccer team noticed her and connected Sabrita with an agent who provided her with an opportunity to play in Israel. Playing for a European league was another one of Sabrita's dreams and it looked like it was also starting to come to fruition! She has also been approached by other leagues but she opted to stay with the Israeli team.

Sabrita has been able to support her family and help her father with all their expenses. She would send money to them every month and finance her siblings' education.

Lessons from Sabrita's Journey:

1. **Believe in Yourself:** Sabitra's story emphasizes the importance of self-belief. No matter where you start, trust in your dreams and abilities.
2. **Persistence Pays Off:** Facing challenges is an opportunity in disguise. Keep working hard, and eventually, you'll break through obstacles.
3. **Inspire Others:** Once you achieve your dreams, be sure to inspire the next generation. Serve as a mentor and a beacon of hope for those who follow in your footsteps.
4. **Dream Big:** Sabitra's journey reminds us that there are no limits to your dreams. Aim high and work diligently to reach your goals.

5. **Embrace Challenges:** Challenges and setbacks are part of the journey to success. Embrace them, learn from them, and use them to grow stronger.

6. **Step out of Your Comfort Zone:** To achieve great things, you often have to leave your comfort zone. Explore new opportunities and be willing to adapt to different situations.

7. **Balance Is Key:** Balancing responsibilities, whether it's education or other commitments, is crucial to achieving your dreams. Stay organized and manage your time effectively.

Sabitra Bhandari's remarkable journey teaches us that determination, hard work, and a belief in oneself can lead to incredible achievements, regardless of the challenges faced. Her story is a source of inspiration and motivation for all.

MO ISOM

"What you are doing in the dark is ultimately affecting your heart."

- Mo Isom

Mo Isom, a person known for her never-give-up attitude, has shown us how believing in ourselves and staying strong in tough times can make a huge difference. In this story, we'll take a closer look at Mo's life, highlighting the tough obstacles she faced and how they helped her become the inspiring person she is today.

Mary Morlan Isom, more commonly known as "Mo", was born on October 25, 1989 in Atlanta, Georgia but grew up in a nearby city called Marietta with her parents. From a young age, Mo displayed an incredible passion for sports. Her love for soccer was palpable, and she knew from the start that she wanted to pursue it with all her heart.

Mo went to Lassiter High School in Georgia and excelled in soccer. She won many awards for their team. Mo faced a big challenge though — at 6 feet tall, Mo was much taller than most people. This made her feel self-conscious about her appearance. Mo's strong desire for control, wanting to be really good, very pretty, and successful, made her take a path where she got too focused on herself and became really sad.

In her high-pressure and demanding surroundings, she felt the need to have something that she could manage completely and use as a way to feel better. Unfortunately, this turned into an eating problem, called bulimia, that took up a lot of her thoughts and emotions. She would make herself throw up as many as ten times every day. This was a really tough time in her life.

Mo joined the school's soccer team at Louisiana State University where she played as the goalkeeper. She played a big role in the team from 2008 to 2011.

Mo really enjoyed her time at LSU. When she started college, she wasn't entirely sure what to expect, but she ended up falling in love with LSU. The fans were very supportive, the coaches were excellent, and they pushed her to be her best. It really opened her eyes to what it was like to be a college athlete.

One of the most unique and unforgettable things that Mo did was to try out for an SEC football team. She was the first female to ever do that! She tried out for the kicker position, not just once, but two times with the Tigers football team. Mo looked at it as a special chance for her that she wanted to take. It was a different, but fun, experience to work with the men and to be part of their training. A lot of people watched and judged her at that time but she didn't pay attention to them. Mo learned a lot from that experience that has actually affected her life for the better.

In January 3, 2009, tragedy struck as Mo's father took his own life. She was only about a year into her college soccer career at that time. This event was hugely devastating to Mo and she had great difficulty coping with the situation. Mo spent countless days researching suicide — trying to understand how and why someone could do something as drastic as taking their own life. In the end, this event has made Mo stronger as an individual.

Mo once said in an interview, *"The suicide of my father was massive. It changed my trajectory in life. But as weird as it sounds, it's something I'm grateful for. You have to be grateful for adversity, it makes you grow."*

In less than a year after losing her father, Mo went through another life-altering experience. She was in a serious car accident during Thanksgiving break that came very close to taking her life. It happened while she was driving from LSU back to her home state of Georgia where she lives now.

During the drive, Mo lost control of her Jeep. Her car slammed into an embankment, and then, incredibly, it flipped over not just once, but three times, before it crashed into a tree.

The impact of the crash had Mo going in and out of consciousness. Thankfully, a retired Navy paramedic happened to be passing by, and he rushed to help her. This person's quick thinking and knowledge of first aid played a vital role in saving Mo's life during this very traumatic experience. It's a great example of how sometimes, in the most challenging moments, there are people who come to our aid and make all the difference.

Surrounded by debris during the car accident, Mo shares how she felt the presence of the Holy Spirit. This made her see that life is a lot more significant and meaningful than we often realize. Mo believes that it was during this difficult event that she had a profound realization and found a strong connection with God. It's like the accident opened her eyes to the deeper meaning of life and made her faith in God even stronger.

After going through a challenging rehabilitation process and completing her soccer career at LSU, Mo embarked on a new journey. She began to travel not only across the United States but around the world to share her incredible story. In 2012, she established a speaking ministry, and her story quickly gained national media attention. People were drawn to her story of suffering, resilience, and faith, as well as her remarkable accomplishments in the world of sports.

Lessons from Mo's Journey:

1. **Follow Your Passion:** Mo's unwavering love for soccer allowed her to overcome obstacles and pursue her dreams, regardless of naysayers. She even tried out for the male football team just because she knows she can, and she was out to prove it!

2. **Persistence Pays Off:** Mo's resilience in the face of adversity demonstrated the power of determination and hard work in achieving one's goals.

3. **Turning Pain into Power:** Mo's ability to transform personal grief and pain into motivation serves as a reminder that challenging experiences can fuel personal growth.

4. **The Power of Faith:** Mo's strong faith and reliance on her beliefs helped her navigate life's challenges and find strength during difficult times.

5. **Inspire and Empower Others:** Mo's commitment to empowering and inspiring those around her shows that our personal journeys can positively influence the lives of others.

6. **Finding Purpose:** Mo's journey highlights how facing and overcoming challenges can lead to discovering one's true purpose and calling in life.

Today, Mo lives in the state of Georgia alongside her husband, Jeremiah Aiken. They've created a loving home where they share their lives and dreams together. Mo's journey has transformed her into a motivational figure, and her impact is felt all across the United States. She travels the country, going from place to place, giving inspirational speeches to audiences from all walks of life.

People from far and wide come to hear her miraculous story of resilience, faith, and determination. Mo's narrative is not just about overcoming adversity; it's also about living according to the principles and teachings found in God's word. Her ability to convey the message of faith, hope, and the strength to rise above challenges has made her a beacon of inspiration for countless individuals. She continues to spread her message of perseverance and faith, helping people find their own strength and purpose in life.

LIONEL MESSI

"I start early, and I stay late, day after day, year after year, it took me 17 years and 114 days to become an overnight success." –
Lionel Messi

Lionel Messi, often regarded as one of the greatest football players of all time, has had an incredible journey from a young boy in Rosario, Argentina, to becoming a global sports icon. His story is one of perseverance, passion, and unwavering determination. In this biography, we'll delve into the life of Lionel Messi, focusing on the challenges and struggles he faced on his path to success.

Lionel Andrés Messi, aka Lionel Messi, also called Leo Messi was born on June 24, 1987 tp a humble, working family in Rosario, Argentina. His father was a factory steel worker, and his mother a cleaner.

When Leo was just a little kid, he loved soccer so much that he didn't let anything hold him back. He would play soccer with his two older brothers and their friends who were much bigger and older. He would run alongside them, dribbling the ball with a determination that was way beyond his years.

Leo was 8 years old when he got picked to join the youth team of a soccer club called Newell's Old Boys. Imagine how exciting that must have been for a young Leo! This was his first step on the path to becoming a soccer legend, and it all started right in his hometown. So, at a very young age, he was already on his way to making his dreams come true.

Leo has always been the shortest among his age group. Eventually, at 11 years old, he was diagnosed by doctors as suffering from a hormone deficiency that restricted his growth. Because of this deficiency, Leo would have to have nightly hormone injections to help him grow taller and stronger, which was important for a soccer player.

Leo's parents did everything they could to help him. They gave him those growth-hormone injections every night. But here's the thing — the medicine wasn't cheap! It costs several hundred dollars every single month! That's a lot of money for most families, and Leo's family wasn't any different. They didn't have a lot of money, but they loved their son and believed in his dreams.

One local club, River Plate, noticed his talent and wanted to sign him up to play for them but they didn't want to pay for his medical treatment. At 13 years old, he had a chance to prove himself with one of the biggest clubs in the world – Barcelona. He went for a trial with Barcelona, and the coach, Carles Rexach, was very impressed with what he saw. He saw something special in Leo, something that made him stand out on the soccer field.

Coach Rexach, right there in a little café, offered Leo a contract (written on a paper napkin!) to join Barcelona. Even more incredible, the contract included something very important: Barcelona would pay for Leo's medical treatment in Spain! This was a huge deal because it meant that he could keep getting the help he needed to grow. So, Leo and his dad packed their bags and moved to Barcelona to become a part of FC Barcelona's youth academy.

Leo scored 21 goals in 14 games and moved up the ranks in the junior soccer system pretty quickly while still missing his home in Argentina. In spite of his short stature, Leo's speed and relentless attacking style has made him the player to watch out for. At 16 years old, he was given his informal debut with FB Barcelona in a friendly match.

Leo was the youngest player to ever score a goal for FC Barcelona. He led his team to a myriad of awards, most notably in 2009 when they captured the Champions League, La Liga, and Spanish Super Cup titles. That same year, Leo took home his first FIFA World Player of the Year award as well as his first Ballon d'Or award, which is the top European individual honor in football.

Leo was the first Argentinian player to bring home the Ballon d'Or award. People have compared him with another famous Argentian soccer player. Remember Diego Maradona? He's one of the best soccer players of all time and was mentioned in this book as well.

Diego was so impressed with Leo's soccer skills and has been quoted saying: *"I have seen the player who will inherit my place in Argentine football and his name is Messi. Messi is a genius, and he can become an even better player. His potential is limitless, and I think he's got everything it takes to become Argentina's greatest player."*

Throughout his amazing professional career, Leo has netted an incredible 815 goals for both his club and country. Notably, he holds the unique record of being the first and solitary player in history to clinch five and six European Golden Shoes. When it comes to soccer honors, Leo stands tall as the most decorated player of all time, with a grand total of 44 collective trophies under his belt. Additionally, he's been honored with a remarkable seven Ballon d'Or awards, a record that sets him apart as the most celebrated footballer in history!

Lessons from Leo's Journey:

1. **Embrace Your Differences:** Leo's journey teaches us that our unique qualities can become our strengths. Rather than being disheartened by his height, he used it to his advantage, developing agility, balance, and control that set him apart on the football field.

AMAZING SOCCER STORIES FOR KIDS

2. **The Power of Family:** Leo's story reminds us of the importance of a strong support system. Our families can be our biggest champions, helping us overcome obstacles and achieve our dreams. His family were his strongest supporters who never gave up on him even with his growth deficiency as a child. They moved with him to Barcelona so he can follow his soccer dreams.

3. **Embrace Opportunities:** Leo's journey to Barcelona shows us that sometimes, we need to leave our comfort zones to pursue our dreams. New opportunities can lead to incredible growth and success.

4. **Resilience in the Face of Setbacks:** Leo's determination to recover from injuries is a testament to the importance of resilience. When life throws obstacles in our path, we must keep pushing forward, learning from setbacks, and never giving up on our dreams.

5. **Believe in Yourself:** Leo's story reminds us that self-belief is essential. Despite what others may say, it's vital to have confidence in your abilities and keep working toward your goals.

Leo's life journey is a testament to the incredible power of determination, resilience, and unwavering self-belief. From his early struggles with a growth hormone deficiency to his multiple injury setbacks and the pressure of international competition, Messi's story is one of overcoming adversity and achieving greatness.

He is a source of inspiration and motivation for young readers. It shows that no matter the obstacles, with determination and the right mindset, anyone can overcome challenges and achieve their dreams.

BERNARD KAMUNGO

"Keep going, we don't stop here. Striving for more and keep working hard every week and try to help out the team every day. Everything is going to come, I believe in hard work and that's what I do in training every day." –

Bernard Kamungo

Amidst the lush landscapes and natural splendor of Tanzania, a remarkable young man named Bernard Kamungo was born in a refugee camp there. His life was a vivid tapestry of challenges and struggles, woven with threads of determination, resilience, and unwavering hope. Here we talk about the challenges young Bernard was born into and how he was able to change his destiny.

In 1996, the 1st Congo War began in the wake of the 1994 Rwandan Genocide. Bernard's family faced unimaginable challenges, as the country descended into chaos. Surviving each day became a struggle as Bernard's parents fought for their very existence.

Because of the war, a refugee camp in western Tanzania was formed. It became a sizable community of 150,000 people as tens of thousands of refugees fled across the border to seek refuge from the civil war in the Democratic Republic of Congo. Bernard's parents were among those people who joined the community in Tanzania. They lived there for about 6 years before Bernard was born in 2002.

In the refugee camp, Bernard would talk to his family in Swahili but also learned to speak French in refugee school. Life was very challenging and his parents worked hard just to make ends meet. It was difficult times but Bernard's family had to be patient while they wait for their turn to be called for resettlement at a different country.

They had limited resources and some days where there would be no food on the table. *"Sometimes I come back from school and my family just wouldn't be able to provide anything," Bernard said.* From a young age, Bernard learned the values of hard work, honesty, and the importance of community.

At such a young age, Bernard understood that life in the camp was tough. At the age of 11, he stopped going to school without telling his parents. Instead, he sold clothes to help buy food for his family. He didn't want to disappoint his parents by telling them that he wasn't going to school every morning.

He loved playing soccer with his friends though. They didn't have any money to buy a soccer ball so they would just make their own out of old clothes wrapped in a medical glove. How creative! Bernard's father used to work at the hospital as a cleaner and would use hospital gloves — that was how Bernard had access to them. Despite not having any formal training or playing in an organized team, Bernard's skills in soccer developed and flourished!

In January of 2017, after more than 2 decades of living and waiting in the refugee camp, it was finally Bernard's family's turn to be resettled to the United States! Bernard was 14 years old at the time and had no idea what life would be like outside the camp. His only dream and expectation was that there would finally be enough food for his whole family!

The whole family arrived in Abilene, TX and for the first time in Bernard's life, they had heat, indoor plumbing, air-conditioning, and a refrigerator stocked with edible food! He remembered feeling so happy and overwhelmed!

Bernard was ecstatic to find out he would be going to Craig Middle School. He was assigned to 8th grade and had to take ESL classes. In spite of difficulty communicating because of language issues, Bernard was just excited to be able to go to school and get free lunches and snacks any time of the day! *"I was first excited knowing that I'll be going to school and get food. You know, like we get a break and eat in the middle of school. And I was like, 'This is amazing. I'll never stop going to school,'"* he said.

He joined the middle school soccer team and dominated! He made so much noise that Abilene High School coach Kyle Riese was already very eager to welcome him into their varsity squad. Bernard didn't disappoint him. He scored multiple goals per game and never failed to win intrasquad scrimmages, no matter who lined up alongside him!

Unfortunately, Abilene isn't known for producing great soccer players. He never attracted many college or professional scouts outside of a few local schools reaching out. But Bernard didn't give up and he was very lucky to have a very supportive brother, Imani, who saw the potential in him. Imani made him realize that there may not be college scholarships, but there were professional open tryouts. They scraped some money together and decided to try out for FC Dallas because it had a lower entry fee.

When Bernard showed up for the tryouts, he felt very intimidated. Everyone there were so serious and very organized. But as soon as Bernard got on the soccer field, he was again able to impress everyone with his skills. The next day, FC Dallas' second team, North Texas Soccer Club, came calling. Kamungo was invited to preseason training!

Bernard worked hard to keep up with the professional players. He knew he needed to improve his speed, tactics, and his fitness. His hard work paid off and he managed to score 22 goals in 52 games, making him one of the on club's all-time leading scorer. He often trained with the first team and occasionally traveled with FC Dallas. He finally made his MLS debut at San Jose in 2022 and was offered a 4 year contract by FC Dallas!

Bernard's life is a testament to the strength of the human spirit and the importance of family. His journey, marked by countless challenges and struggles, reminds us that with determination, resilience, and a steadfast belief in one's dreams, even the most daunting obstacles can be conquered. Bernard's story is an inspiration for young minds, proving that they too can achieve greatness and make a positive impact on the world.

Lessons from Bernard's Journey:

1. **The Power of Family:** The Kamungo family's bond and support for one another is a testament to the importance of family in overcoming adversity. The faith Imani, Bernard's brother, had for Bernard's skills was what pushed Bernard to tryout for a soccer team.
2. **Embracing Change:** Bernard's story teaches us the importance of embracing change and adapting to new environments, even when it seems daunting. Bernard had no idea what it was like to live outside of the refugee camp or trying out for an organized soccer team — but he didn't let fear stop him.

3. **Overcoming Obstacles:** Bernard was born in a refugee camp where life was tough and opportunities were hard to come by but that didn't stop him from

4. **Inspiring Others:** His story shows us that we all have the potential to inspire others and make a difference in the world, regardless of our background or circumstances.

Bernard Kamungo's journey serves as a guiding light for young minds, illuminating the path to success, resilience, and the profound impact they can have on the world, no matter where they come from or what challenges they face.

RIVALDO

"A man without a family has nothing from life. I need my family in order to enjoy life when things are going well. And when things are not going well, they give me support."
- Rivaldo

Rivaldo's journey from a humble background to becoming one of the greatest football players of all time is nothing short of inspiring. Rivaldo Vítor Borba Ferreira, known simply as Rivaldo, was born on April 19, 1972 in Recife, Brazil into a poor working class family. His story began in a challenging environment, where poverty was a constant companion.

Rivaldo's family struggled to make ends meet, and the future seemed uncertain. But from a young age, Rivaldo had a dream: he wanted to play soccer professionally. This dream became his guiding star through the toughest times.

Rivaldo grew up in extreme poverty in one of the toughest *favelas* in Recife. A *favela* means a slum or shantytown located within or on the outskirts of the country's large cities and are usually formed due to squatters setting up homes in the area. *Favelas* are known to be very high in crime and drug-related violence.

Rivaldo's family was so poor that there were days when they wouldn't have any food to eat. Rivaldo became so malnourished that he suffered from bowleggedness and even lost some teeth. In fact, even at present, some of his physical features still show signs of such malnourishment.

Soccer is the most popular sport in Brazil and plays a big part of the country's national identity. Like a lot of the poor Brazilian youths, Rivaldo started his soccer journey early in life and out in the streets. He couldn't afford any soccer gear or even a ball — Rivaldo often played out in the streets barefooted.

Rivaldo's journey into professional soccer was not a walk in the park. He faced many rejections and disappointments early in his career. At times, the world seemed to conspire against him and he was often counted out. But Rivaldo didn't give up. He knew that if he wanted to achieve his dreams, he had to keep pushing himself.

Despite facing many health problems, Rivaldo was a passionate soccer player who thrived as a forward. Back in 1989, when he was just 16 years old, he joined his local team called Paulistano Futebol Clube. Even though the coaches thought he might be too frail to play soccer, Rivaldo showed them they were mistaken.

That same year, Rivaldo faced a tough time when he lost his dad, Romildo Ferreira, in a car accident. However, this sad event didn't stop him from chasing his dream of becoming a soccer player. That very year, he took a big step toward his dream by signing up with Paulistano Futebol Clube as a professional player.

It was hard not to notice Rivaldo's amazing soccer skills. He soon caught the eye of bigger clubs like Palmeiras and Corinthians. This was a big moment in his soccer journey. When he joined Palmeiras, something incredible happened – they won the Brazilian Championship in 1994. This was a really big deal, especially for a young player like Rivaldo! It showed that he was not just good but one of the best players in Brazil.

In 1996, Rivaldo made the big leap to European football when he signed with Deportivo La Coruña in Spain. This was no easy task as he had to play in a completely new continent. Rivaldo embraced the challenge, proving that he was more than capable of competing at the highest level.

One of the most defining moments in Rivaldo's career was his transfer to FC Barcelona in 1997. At Barcelona, he joined a team with exceptional players like Luis Figo and Ronaldo. The competition was fierce, but Rivaldo's dedication and incredible skill shone through.

Rivaldo played a big role in helping Brazil reach the final of the 1998 World Cup in France. He scored three goals during the tournament then the next year, he scored 5 goals as

Brazil won the Copa America again in Bolivia. It's like he was a superhero for Brazil's soccer team! In 2002, Rivaldo had his finest moment as a footballer as he scored five goals in the World Cup to help Brazil win their record 5th title!

While Rivaldo enjoyed immense success throughout his career, he faced some difficult moments as well. Injuries and changing team dynamics led to a decline in his performance. He moved between clubs, including Milan and Olympiacos, but the challenges only increased with time.

In 2015, Rivaldo officially retired from professional soccer. His legacy as one of the greatest players in the sport was well-established. After his playing career, he remained connected to the world of soccer, mentoring young players and contributing to the sport's growth.

Rivaldo's journey from a challenging childhood to becoming a soccer legend is a testament to the power of perseverance, determination, and a strong support system. His story is an inspiration for young readers, showing them that with hard work and a never-give-up attitude, they can achieve their dreams, no matter how big or small.

Lessons from Rivaldo's Journey:

1. **Dream Big, Start Small:** Rivaldo's story teaches us that it's essential to have a dream, no matter how big or small. Your dreams can be your motivation, pushing you to work hard, even when the odds seem stacked against you.

2. **Embrace Failure as a Stepping Stone:** Rivaldo's story reminds us that failure is not the end; it's a stepping stone to success. Each rejection, each setback, is an opportunity to learn and grow.

3. **Be Ambitious:** Don't be afraid to aim for the stars. Even if your current circumstances are less than ideal, setting high goals can motivate you to work harder and reach new heights.

4. **Hard Work Pays Off:** Success doesn't happen overnight. Rivaldo's path from the youth team to a championship-winning squad required dedication and hard work. He didn't just rely on his talent; he continued to improve his skills.

5. **Never Stop Learning:** Surrounding yourself with people who are better than you can be a powerful motivator for improvement. Rivaldo learned from his teammates and pushed himself to become even better.

6. **Persevere Through Adversity:** Even in the face of adversity, Rivaldo continued to fight for his dreams. His story teaches us the importance of resilience when facing difficult times.

Rivaldo's life is a living example of these lessons, and by applying them to your own life, you can overcome challenges and achieve your goals. Remember, every legend was once an ordinary person who refused to give up on their dreams.

MARTA

"We all have obstacles. The feeling of satisfaction comes by overcoming something."
- **Marta**

Marta Vieira da Silva, more commonly known as Marta, is a name synonymous with soccer excellence. From the small fields of her native Brazil to the grand stadiums of the world, she has left an indelible mark on the sport. Her life story is one of challenges, struggles, and unyielding determination.

Marta is often regarded as the greatest female soccer player of all time. She has been named FIFA World Player of the Year six times (five in a row from 2006 through 2010) and the latest award coming in 2018. Her journey to greatness has not been easy as she had to face several challenges in her childhood including financial difficulties and gender stereotypes.

Marta was born on February 19, 1986, in the small town of Dois Riachos, in northeastern Brazil. Marta's father left them when she was still a baby leaving her mother behind to raise Marta and her 3 siblings all by herself. Life was difficult and there had certainly been times when meals were hard to come by.

Marta's mother was a cleaning lady and Marta's brother worked at an early age, acting as the father figure in the family. At 7 years old, Marta would sell ice cream and fruit juices to help make some money for their family. She would borrow her uncle's wheelbarrow to carry people's groceries in the market on weekends just to make some small change. She has also helped a shoe keeper sell clothing items in exchange for a pair of socks. She would keep the money and offer to split some of the bills with her mother or use it to buy a pair of sneakers.

When Marta's mother was away at work, Marta would play street soccer with her cousins. She would play with older and bigger boys and still managed to outsmart and outplay them. She realized that she was actually very good and her passion for the sport just grew stronger. Her dream to become a professional soccer player was born. She also thought it could be an opportunity for her to help her family come out of poverty.

Marta was the only girl in town who played soccer. Her mother continued to support her in spite of all the disapproval from the community. In Brazil, a country known for its soccer legends, it wasn't easy for a girl like Marta to break into the world of professional soccer. She faced discrimination, both for her gender and her size. People doubted her abilities, but Marta proved them wrong.

If the boys prevented her from playing with them, it didn't stop Marta. She continued to practice by kicking old, deflated soccer balls and even used crumpled grocery bags as makeshift balls on the streets of her tiny hometown. Marta also played barefooted in the streets.

She eventually joined a local boys' junior team and worked tirelessly to improve her skills. At age 14, she was discovered by a scout from Vasco da Gama, a popular men's football club in Rio de Janeiro, and they were looking to start a women's team!

Determined to seize this opportunity, Marta traveled for hours to participate. The competition was fierce, but Marta's skill and passion shone through. She earned a spot on the team, but the challenges were far from over.

Marta's journey from her small Brazilian town to international stardom was paved with countless hurdles. She faced financial struggles, often not having enough money to afford proper equipment or transportation to games and training. Despite this, she continued to rise through the ranks.

Marta first gained widespread notice during her time with Umeå. She led the club to the Union of European Football Associations (UEFA) Women's Cup (now known as the Women's Champions League) title in 2004 and continued to perform and bring their team to the finals until 2008.

Marta's big break came when she was just 17. She was selected to represent Brazil in the 2003 FIFA Women's World Cup. It was a defining moment in her career. She dazzled the world with her extraordinary skills and scored goals that left fans and opponents in awe. Brazil reached the final, but they didn't win. However, Marta's resilience remained unbroken.

After the World Cup, Marta's name became synonymous with soccer excellence. She went on to play for several top clubs around the world and continued to rewrite the record books, proving that gender should never be a barrier to greatness.

Throughout her career, Marta made it a point to empower others. She used her platform to advocate for gender equality in sports and fought against the stereotypes that limited women's opportunities in soccer. Marta's voice became a symbol of hope for girls around the world who dreamt of following in her footsteps.

In 2019, Marta delivered a powerful speech at the FIFA Best Awards. She urged the world to support women's soccer and encouraged young players to believe in their dreams. Her words echoed loudly, motivating the next generation to pursue their passions with unwavering dedication.

Lessons from Marta's Journey:

1. **Passion and Dedication:** Marta's passion for soccer was unwavering. She dedicated herself to her craft, never allowing obstacles to deter her from her dreams. Her story teaches us that when you truly love something, nothing can stop you from pursuing it.

2. **Belief in Yourself:** Marta never doubted her abilities, even when others did. She believed in herself and her potential, proving that self-confidence is a powerful tool for success.

3. **Perseverance:** Throughout her career, Marta faced injuries, financial struggles, and discrimination. But she persevered, never giving up on her goals. Her story reminds us that setbacks are a part of life, but they don't have to define us.

4. **Empowering Others:** Marta used her success to advocate for change and empower young players. Her story teaches us the importance of giving back and being a positive influence in the lives of others.

Marta's life journey is a testament to the power of resilience and determination. From humble beginnings to international stardom, she overcame countless challenges to become one of the greatest soccer players in history. Her legacy extends beyond the field, inspiring generations of young athletes to chase their dreams, no matter the obstacles they may face. Marta's story reminds us that with passion, self-belief, perseverance, and a commitment to empowering others, we can achieve greatness in our own lives.

NADIA NADIM

"I have one goal in life; I want to be the best in everything I do."
- **Nadia Nadim**

This is the remarkable story of a young girl who faced incredible challenges and struggles, only to emerge as an inspiring soccer player and a symbol of hope for countless others. As we delve into her life, remember that Nadia's journey will teach you valuable lessons that you can carry with you throughout your own life.

Nadia was born in Herat, Afghanistan on January 2, 1988. She was raised by her mother and father, along with her four sisters. Her father was an officer in the Afghan military. When Nadia was 10 years old, her father was tragically killed by the Taliban.

After this incident, Nadia's family has lived in fear. There are 6 women in their family and they all decided it wasn't safe for them to stay in Afghanistan. Nadia's family was left with no choice but to flee their homeland in search of safety and a better life. Nadia's mother made the difficult decision to flee to London, where they had relatives. She sold most of her valuables, created fake passports, and paid a smuggler to take them to Italy via Pakistan.

When their family reached Italy, they had to ride a truck that was supposed to take them to London. A few days passed and they finally reached their destination — or so they thought — it turned out they were dropped off in Denmark instead! This country has become their new home.

It was a difficult transition for Nadia as she faced language barriers, cultural differences, and a sense of being a stranger in a foreign land. However, she and her family held on to the hope of a brighter future. Nadia was drawn to soccer from a young age. It was on the soccer field where she felt most at home, and it provided her with a means to fit into her new community.

Nadia's journey in Danish soccer began with her local club, B52 Aalborg. She faced the challenges of being a girl in a predominantly male sport, where stereotypes and gender biases often stood in her way. Despite this, she never gave up. She trained harder, played smarter, and exhibited unparalleled determination.

Nadia's talent on the pitch was undeniable, and she soon joined the youth academy of the famous Danish club, Skovbakken from 2006 to 2012. Finally, she joined the Fortuna Hjørring in 2012 where she made her Champions League debut. In that game, Nadia scored all the goals for her team and beat Scottish champions Glasgow City with a score of 2-1.

While playing for Fortuna Hjørring, Nadia was discovered by scouts from the Danish national team. This was a turning point in her life. Her skills earned her a spot on the national

AMAZING SOCCER STORIES FOR KIDS

team, and she wore the red and white jersey with pride. She became the symbol of hope for girls who aspired to play soccer, showing them that gender should never be a barrier to following their dreams.

Despite her budding soccer career, Nadia always recognized the importance of education. She studied medicine at the University of Aarhus in Denmark, proving that you can be both a scholar and an athlete. Nadia's dedication to her studies exemplifies the importance of balancing one's dreams with a solid education.

Throughout her career, Nadia Nadim used her platform to inspire others. She became an advocate for gender equality in sports and worked to remove the barriers that young girls face when pursuing their dreams. Her story is a testament to the power of perseverance, dedication, and self-belief.

Lessons from Nadia's Journey:

1. **Resilience:** Nadia's journey was filled with obstacles, but she never gave up. When life knocks you down, get up, and keep going. Remember, the greatest successes often come after the toughest challenges.
2. **Determination:** Nadia's determination to succeed in soccer, despite the odds stacked against her, is a

lesson in the importance of setting goals and working tirelessly to achieve them.

3. **Balance:** Nadia demonstrated that it's possible to excel in both sports and education. Balancing your passions with a strong education can provide a safety net for the future.

4. **Advocacy:** Using her platform to fight for gender equality, Nadia showed the importance of standing up for what you believe in and making a positive impact on the world.

5. **Believe in Yourself:** No matter where you come from or what challenges you face, believing in yourself is the first step to success. Nadia's story is a testament to the power of self-belief.

CONCLUSION

And that's a wrap, soccer superstars!

We've kicked, dribbled, and cheered our way through the pages of "Amazing Soccer Stories for Kids." Wasn't it a blast?! From jaw-dropping goals to friendships that are as strong as goalie gloves, we've shared some seriously awesome adventures together.

As we close this chapter, remember: just like the coolest soccer moves, life's challenges might try to tackle you, but with heart and a bit of teamwork, you can always score a winning goal! So, keep dreaming big, practice those fancy footwork skills, and never forget that every setback is just a setup for an epic comeback.

Thanks for joining me on this soccer-filled ride. Until next time, kick on, champs!

THANK YOU

Dear Young Reader and Parents,

I want to express my deepest gratitude for choosing my book among the many options out there. As you've journeyed through its pages, I can't thank you enough for your time and trust.

Before your next reading journey, could I ask a small favor? Would you consider sharing your thoughts in a review? For independent authors like myself, your feedback is invaluable and the easiest way to show support. It's through your insights that I can keep crafting books that resonate with you and bring the results you seek. Your words would mean everything to me.

Scan the QR code below to leave a review on Amazon:

US Readers UK Readers

With heartfelt thanks,

Leigh Jordyn

Discover more books in the series!

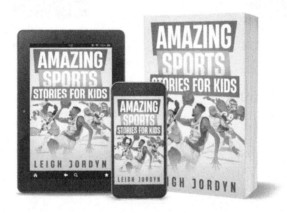

Don't miss out and scan this **QR code** now!

SCAN ME

RESOURCES

Hindustan Times. (2022, December 30). *The Legend Of Pele: How a kid who practiced with jackfruits became a wizard of football* [Video]. YouTube. https://www.youtube.com/watch?v=gfBXJJSo4N4

Rt. (2022, December 30). Pele: From humble beginnings to football's first global superstar. *RT International.* https://www.rt.com/sport/567753-pele-obituary-life-career/

Osborn, C. (2022, December 29). Pelé, who made soccer "The Beautiful Game," dies at 82 | WBUR. *WBUR.org.* https://www.wbur.org/npr/993143216/pele-brazil-soccer-superstar-dies

Cristiano Ronaldo Quotes (Author of Moments by Ronaldo, Cristiano (2007) paperback). (n.d.).

https://www.goodreads.com/author/quotes/653078.Cri
stiano_Ronaldo

Cristiano Ronaldo. (2023, March 7). *Biography.*
https://www.biography.com/athletes/cristiano-ronaldo

Rollin, J. (2023, October 8). *Cristiano Ronaldo / Biography
& Facts.* Encyclopedia Britannica.
https://www.britannica.com/biography/Cristiano-
Ronaldo

Medical Tourism Mexico. (n.d.). *Cristiano Ronaldo's heart
surgery at 15: an unexpected turn.*
https://www.medicaltourismex.com/article/cristiano-
ronaldo-heart-surgery-at-15-years-
old#:~:text=Cristiano%20Ronaldo%2C%20renowned
%20as%20one,about%20his%20future%20in%20fo
otball.

TOP 25 QUOTES BY DIEGO MARADONA / A-Z Quotes.
(n.d.). A-Z Quotes.
https://www.azquotes.com/author/9430-
Diego_Maradona

Soccer Stories - Oh My Goal. (2020, November 27).
*Before you lose hope, watch Diego Maradona's
childhood story / Oh My Goal* [Video]. YouTube.
https://www.youtube.com/watch?v=qOwN1JxUmiQ

The Editors of Encyclopaedia Britannica. (2023, September 21). *Diego Maradona | Biography, Hand of God, & Facts*. Encyclopedia Britannica. https://www.britannica.com/biography/Diego-Maradona

Diego Maradona. (2023, September 6). *Biography*. https://www.biography.com/athletes/diego-maradona

30 Best Carlos Tevez Quotes With Image | Bookey. (2023, September 21). *https://www.bookey.app/quote-author/carlos-tevez*. https://www.bookey.app/quote-author/carlos-tevez

Daily Dose Of Football. (2020, October 17). *Just how GOOD was Carlos Tevez Actually?* [Video]. YouTube. https://www.youtube.com/watch?v=2x4u7ax1RH4

Hendrix, H. (2023). Carlos Tevez Childhood Story plus Untold Biography Facts. *LifeBogger*. https://lifebogger.com/carlos-tevez/

Biography and City Career. (n.d.). Mancity. https://www.mancity.com

Who is Carlos Tevez? Everything You Need to Know. (n.d.). https://www.thefamouspeople.com/profiles/carlos-tevez-11735.php

30 Best Sadio Mane Quotes With Image I Bookey. (2019). *Bookey Book Summary*. https://www.bookey.app/quote-author/sadio-mane

Hendrix, H. (2023b). Sadio Mane Childhood Story plus Untold Biography Facts. *LifeBogger*. https://lifebogger.com/sadio-mane-childhood-story-plus-untold-biography-facts/

November, A. B. I. C. 2. (2022, November 2). Sadio Mané: The Senagalese football star that favours human touch over sporting goals. *Olympics.com*. https://olympics.com/en/news/how-sadio-mane-favours-human-touch-over-football

ONOME EBI @ebionome. (2023, June 15). [Video]. Twitter. https://twitter.com/EBIONOME/status/1669327537112064000?ref_src=twsrc%5Etfw

Abadi, J. (2023, July 30). Onome Ebi biography – Career, salary, net worth, awards. *GoalBall Live*. https://goalballlive.com/onome-ebi-biography-career-salary-net-worth-awards/

Chukwurah, F. (2021, January 25). Nigerian football legend Onome Ebi helping next generation. *dw.com*. https://www.dw.com/en/football-legend-onome-ebi-helping-next-generation-of-nigerian-female-footballers/a-56319540

Michael, M. U. (2023). Onome EBi Husband, family, parents, children, siblings, father, mother, sister & brother. *Uzomedia TV.* https://uzomediatv.com/onome-ebi-husband-family-parents-children-siblings-father-mother-sister-brother/

Wikipedia contributors. (2023i). Victor Moses. *Wikipedia.* https://en.wikipedia.org/wiki/Victor_Moses#:~:text=Moses%20was%20born%20in%20Lagos,the%20UK%20to%20claim%20asylum.

Hendrix, H. (2023c). Victor Moses Childhood Story plus Untold Biography Facts. *LifeBogger.* https://lifebogger.com/victor-moses-childhood-story-plus-untold-biography-facts/

Stets, R. (2022). Victor Moses: what happened to his parents and how did he achieve international success? *Legit.ng - Nigeria News.* https://www.legit.ng/1154364-victor-moses-parents-biography-career.html

Who is Victor Moses? Everything You Need to Know. (n.d.). https://www.thefamouspeople.com/profiles/victor-moses-36112.php

BabaGol. (2021). One Brave Kat: An interview with
Katayoun Khosrowyar — BabaGol. *BabaGol.*
https://www.babagol.net/blog/2018/8/10/one-brave-
kat

Funk, R. T. (2020). Katayoun Khosrowyar; The Iranian
Coach on A Mission — REFORM THE FUNK. *REFORM
THE FUNK.*
https://www.reformthefunk.com/features/katayoun-
khosrowyar-the-iranian-coach-on-a-mission

Aarons, E. (2018, June 20). 'The fact we exist is huge':
Iran's women plotting course to world stage. *The
Guardian.*
https://www.theguardian.com/football/2018/jun/20/ira
n-women-kat-khosrowyar-fifa

Afc, T. (2020, June 1). Sabitha Bhandari's journey from
barefoot dreamer to Nepal dazzler. *the-AFC.*
https://www.the-
afc.com/en/more/news/sabitha_bhandaris_journey_fro
m_barefoot_dreamer_to_nepal_dazzler.html

Sunam, A. (2020, February 7). From barefoot player to
wonder striker, the rise of Nepal's Sabitra Bhandari. . .
The New Indian Express.
https://www.newindianexpress.com/sport/football/202

0/feb/07/from-barefoot-player-to-wonder-striker-the-rise-of-nepals-sabitra-bhandari-2100289.html

Sangroula, P. (2023, July 20). Sabitra Bhandari: South Asia's best looking to take the Israeli league by storm - OnlineKhabar English. *OnlineKhabar English News.* https://english.onlinekhabar.com/sabitra-bhandari-israeli-women-league.html

Cyriac, B. B. (2020, February 15). Nepal's Sabitra atop Indian women's football summit. *The Times of India.* https://timesofindia.indiatimes.com/sports/football/top-stories/nepals-sabitra-atop-indian-womens-football-summit/articleshow/74152490.cms

Amber. (2023, May 21). *38: Mo Isom / Sex, Jesus, and The Conversations The Church Forgot -.* https://www.graceenoughpodcast.com/38-mo-isom-sex-jesus-and-the-conversations-the-church-forgot/#:~:text=%22He%20will%20wreck%20your%20life,your%20heart%20and%20your%20life.%22

Okeke, V., Okeke, V., & Okeke, V. (2023, January 27). *Mo Isom Aiken: Biography, Age, Family Life, Career, And Net Worth.* Naijapage - Pastors, Devotionals, Online Sermons, Prayers and Christian News.

https://naijapage.com/mo-iso-aiken-biography-age-family-life-career-and-net-worth/

Wikipedia contributors. (2022, April 3). *Mo isom.* Wikipedia. https://en.wikipedia.org/wiki/Mo_Isom

Froyd, C. (2017, January 25). Former LSU soccer star Mo Aiken-Isom shares her incredible story. *Death Valley Voice.* https://deathvalleyvoice.com/2017/01/25/former-lsu-soccer-star-mo-aiken-isom-shares-her-incredible-story/#:~:text=Isom%20began%20her%20LSU%20career,really%20loved%20my%20time%20there.

Tooby, D. (2023, April). *33 SOCCER QUOTES FROM LIONEL MESSI (INSPIRATIONAL).* Progressive Soccer. https://www.progressivesoccertraining.com/soccer-quotes-lionel-messi/

Donica, A. (2023, September 12). Lionel Messi. *Biography.* https://www.biography.com/athletes/lionel-messi

Karmakar, S. (2022, December 21). Lionel Messi Was Diagnosed With Growth Hormone Disorder At 11: How Argentina Football Legend Overcame It I. *TheHealthSite.* https://www.thehealthsite.com/diseases-conditions/lionel-messi-was-diagnosed-with-growth-hormone-disorder-at-11-how-argentina-football-legend-overcame-it-936503/

Lionel Messi Biography / (2022, November 30). Biography Online. https://www.biographyonline.net/sport/football/lionel-messi.html

Rollin, J. (2023b, October 21). *Lionel Messi / Biography, Barcelona, PSG, & Facts*. Encyclopedia Britannica. https://www.britannica.com/biography/Lionel-Messi

Wikipedia contributors. (2023j, October 22). *List of career achievements by Lionel Messi*. Wikipedia. https://en.wikipedia.org/wiki/List_of_career_achievements_by_Lionel_Messi#:~:text=He%20has%20scored%20815%20goals,total%20of%2044%20collective%20trophies.

Dallas, F. (2023, April 16). FC Dallas Roars to Victory over Real Salt Lake. *FC Dallas*. https://www.fcdallas.com/news/fc-dallas-roars-to-victory-over-real-salt-lake

Muzinga, T. (2023, October 3). FC Dallas' Bernard Kamungo shares inspiring story of humble beginnings. *FOX 4 News Dallas-Fort Worth*.

https://www.fox4news.com/sports/fc-dallas-bernard-kamungo-shares-inspiring-story-of-humble-beginnings

Piellucci, M. (2023, June 30). *Straight Out of Tanzania: Bernard Kamungo's Once-In-a-Lifetime Journey to FC Dallas.* D Magazine. https://www.dmagazine.com/sports/2023/06/straight-out-of-tanzania-bernard-kamungos-once-in-a-lifetime-journey-to-fc-dallas/

Davis, S. (2023, August 1). Steve Davis: Bernard Kamungo is seizing his chance with remarkable opportunism. *FC Dallas.* https://www.fcdallas.com/news/steve-davis-bernard-kamungo-is-seizing-his-chance-with-remarkable-opportunism

81 Rivaldo - Inspiring quotes at Quote.org. (n.d.). https://quote.org/author/rivaldo-67857

Wikipedia contributors. (2023k, October 26). *Rivaldo.* Wikipedia. https://en.wikipedia.org/wiki/Rivaldo#:~:text=9%20Ext ernal%20links-,Early%20life,the%20loss%20of%20several%20teeth.

The Editors of Encyclopaedia Britannica. (2023b, October 13). *Rivaldo / Biography & Facts.* Encyclopedia

Britannica. https://www.britannica.com/biography/Rivaldo

Who is Rivaldo? Everything You Need to Know. (n.d.). https://www.thefamouspeople.com/profiles/rivaldo-6848.php

Baxter, K. (2014, June 10). In streets of Brazil, the soul of soccer is a long way from World Cup - Los Angeles Times. *Los Angeles Times.* https://www.latimes.com/sports/soccer/la-sp-world-cup-brazil-kids-20140610-story.html

Marta quotes. (n.d.). BrainyQuote. https://www.brainyquote.com/quotes/marta_653891

Marta. (n.d.). Britannica Kids. https://kids.britannica.com/students/article/Marta/635862#:~:text=of%20all%20time.-,Early%20Years,the%20streets%20of%20Dois%20Riachos.

Augustyn, A. (2013, March 13). *Marta / Biography & Facts.* Encyclopedia Britannica. https://www.britannica.com/biography/Marta

Wikipedia contributors. (2023l, October 30). *Marta (footballer).* Wikipedia. https://en.wikipedia.org/wiki/Marta_(footballer)

Brazil's Marta broke down barriers to become one of football's best players. (2019, August 13). CGTN America. https://america.cgtn.com/2019/08/11/brazils-marta-broke-down-barriers-to-become-one-of-footballs-best-players

CGTN America. (2019, August 13). *Brazil's Marta broke down barriers to become one of football's best players* [Video]. YouTube. https://www.youtube.com/watch?v=i7hJgYpqFRM

Nadia Nadim Biography For Kids. (2021, July 7). Lottie Dolls US. https://www.lottie.com/blogs/strong-women/nadia-nadim-biography-for-kids

Wikipedia contributors. (2023k, October 22). *Nadia Nadim.* Wikipedia. https://en.wikipedia.org/wiki/Nadia_Nadim#:~:text=Early%20life%20and%20career,-Nadia%20was%20born&text=When%20Nadim%20was%209%20years,four%20sisters%E2%80%93%20fled%20to%20Denmark.

IMDb. (n.d.-b). *Nadia Nadim.* IMDb. https://www.imdb.com/name/nm9214947/bio/

Made in the USA
Coppell, TX
18 June 2024

33675248R00073